ALONG the RAILS

ALONG the RAILS

THE LORE AND ROMANCE OF THE RAILROAD

Brian Solomon with C. J. Riley

MetroBooks

MetroBooks

An Imprint of Friedman/Fairfax Publishers

©2000 by Michael Friedman Publishing Group, Inc.

Library of Congress Cataloging-in-Publication Data

Solomon, Brian.
   Along the rails : the lore and romance of the railroad /
Brian Solomon ; with C.J. Riley.
   p.   cm.
   Includes bibliographical references.
   ISBN 1-56799-741-4
   1. Railroads—History. I. Riley, C. J., 1942- II. Title.
   HE1021 .s64 1999
   385'.09—dc21   99-26046
                                                     CIP

Editor: Celeste Sollod
Art Director: Jeff Batzli
Designer: Kirsten Wehmann Berger
Illustrations on pp. 6, 10, 36, 58, 76, 104:
© Kirsten Wehmann Berger
Photography Editor: Amy Talluto
Production Manager: Camille Lee

Color separations by Bright Arts Graphics (S) Pte. Ltd.
Printed in China by Leefung-Asco Printers Ltd.

10 9 8 7 6 5 4 3 2 1

For bulk purchases and special sales, please contact:
Friedman/Fairfax Publishers
Attention: Sales Department
15 West 26th Street
New York, New York 10010
212/685-6610   FAX 212/685-1307

Visit our website:
www.metrobooks.com

Acknowledgments

Grateful acknowledgment is given to authors, publishers, and photographers for permission to reprint material. Every effort has been made to determine copyright owners of text, photographs, and illustrations. In the case of any omissions, the publisher will be pleased to make suitable acknowledgments in future editions.

Reprinted by permission of the publishers and the Trustees of Amherst College from *The Poems of Emily Dickinson,* Thomas H. Johnson, ed., Cambridge, Mass.: The Belknap Press of Harvard University Press, Copyright © 1951, 1955, 1979, 1983 by the President and Fellows of Harvard College.

Passage from *To the Great Ocean* by Harmon Tupper. Copyright © 1965 by Herman Tupper and Elsie Tupper. By permission of Little, Brown and Company (Inc.).

"Travel" by Edna St. Vincent Millay. From *Collected Poems,* HarperCollins. Copyright 1921, 1948 by Edna St. Vincent Millay. All rights reserved. Reprinted by permission of Elizabeth Barnett, literary executor.

Contents

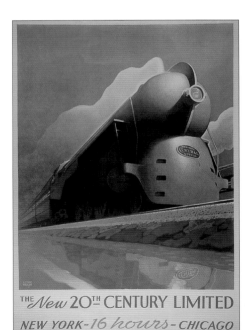

THE *New* 20TH CENTURY LIMITED
NEW YORK - *16 hours* - CHICAGO
NEW YORK CENTRAL SYSTEM

"**T**rains are wonderful.... To travel by train is to see nature and human beings, towns and churches and rivers, in fact, to see life."
—Agatha Christie, *An Autobiography*

ON THE RAILS

The power and romance of the train is undeniable. The steam railway is captivating and entrancing. A product and ultimately an integral component of the industrial revolution, railroads have had a tremendous impact on everyday life.

The railway was born in the north of England during the early nineteenth century and within five decades had spread to nearly every corner of the civilized world. The industry attracted many talented people: insightful visionaries who conceived of ever better ways to transport goods and people; engineers who overcame technical challenges; businessmen and financiers who raised capital to build the lines and locomotives; able-bodied laborers who risked life and limb to construct the right of way, tracks, and structures that comprise the railway infrastructure; and the brave railroaders themselves, the people who operated the trains. Railroading is a dangerous business, and those involved have had innumerable adventures in the course of carrying out their daily duties. Those adventures form the base of this fascinating collection of railroad lore: tales of daring, danger, triumph, and tragedy.

The railroading industry has developed an astonishingly rich culture and lore in a relatively short span of time. In the course of less than two hundred years, the railways have inspired thousands of stories. Railroaders have developed a distinctive lingo, creating a unique language. Railroad lore is far more than just a historical accounting of railroad building and operations; it includes the intrigue, the myths, the songs, the poems, and even the advertising slogans that embrace the railroad culture and its people, trains, locomotives, stations, and tracks. Railroad lore is the work of thousands of storytellers, photographers, songwriters, and poets. It is made up of the combined experience of everyone who has ever been touched by the railroad.

The colorful and eclectic text in this volume touches on some of the highlights of a rich and vivid industry—one that is still very much alive in most parts of the world, and continues to create new stories every day.

PAGE 7: Even everyday passenger trains shone with glory during the railroad's golden age, when there was no finer way to travel than on a train. OPPOSITE: The Canadian Pacific reached from coast to coast, unifying the vast Dominion of Canada, from the busy ports of the East to the grand mountains of the West.

Chapter One

Over the Hill and Through the Woods

Building the Railways

In the nineteenth century, railroads were cutting-edge technology. To some the railway was fresh and exciting; it represented progress and hope. But to others the railway was a terrifying new force that threatened the very fabric of society. Regardless of personal perspective, the railways brought about enormous changes, and railroad pioneers had to buck convention and placate opponents and critics to make their dreams reality. Thousands of men and millions of dollars were required to construct the railways, and simply securing the capital to accomplish the most basic tasks was often a Herculean feat. Why would anyone risk money on a radical, unproven method of transport? Even after the industry was long established, financing could prove a serious obstacle. The railway lines had to be surveyed, rights of way secured, bridges erected and tunnels bored, tracks put down, and buildings constructed. Locomotives had to be developed; systems of operation and control were refined and perfected.

While the railway originated in England, railroad technology was quickly adopted by many other nations and railways were built around the world, so there are tales of triumph and tragedy on the steel rails from all over. From the Rocky Mountains of North America to the Falkland Islands in the Atlantic, every area offers its own distinctive lore about the construction and maintenance of the railroad.

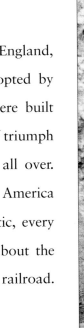

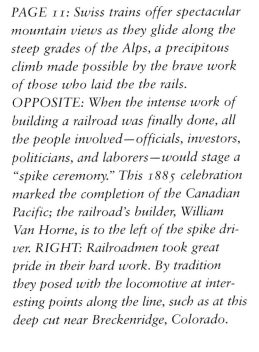

PAGE 11: Swiss trains offer spectacular mountain views as they glide along the steep grades of the Alps, a precipitous climb made possible by the brave work of those who laid the the rails.
OPPOSITE: When the intense work of building a railroad was finally done, all the people involved—officials, investors, politicians, and laborers—would stage a "spike ceremony." This 1885 celebration marked the completion of the Canadian Pacific; the railroad's builder, William Van Horne, is to the left of the spike driver. RIGHT: Railroadmen took great pride in their hard work. By tradition they posed with the locomotive at interesting points along the line, such as at this deep cut near Breckenridge, Colorado.

The First Steam Passenger Train

"I fully expect to get the [steam] engine introduced on the Darlington Railway."

—George Stephenson in an 1821 letter to William James,

from the book *George Stephenson: The Engineer and His Letters.*

ABOVE: George Stephenson's Stockton & Darlington was the first public railway to embrace the locomotive, a curious, crudely constructed contraption during the railroad's formative period.
OPPOSITE: Preceded by a jubilant flagman on horseback, the very first steam-powered train officially opens Stephenson's famous Stockton & Darlington railway in the north of England.

On September 27, 1825, thousands of people gathered in Shildon, England, to witness the inauguration of service on the world's first steam-powered public railway—the Stockton & Darlington, which was to run in the north of England from the coal fields near Bishop Auckland to Stockton-on-Tees. It was a gala event that would change the way the world thought about transportation.

This first public steam railway had had to surmount tremendous political opposition, technical problems, and financial difficulties before it was ready to make this celebratory run. Railway technology was in its infancy, and not yet accepted as a mode of transportation. While some hoped it would succeed, others wished it would fail. The concept of steam-powered trains was unpalatable to those who did not want them disrupting the landscape and to others who had financial interests in canals and horse-drawn carriages—systems that railways threatened to supersede. While some may have been concerned for the well-being of society, others were just plain selfish. The Earl of Darlington had opposed the line simply because it infringed upon his fox hunting grounds. Ultimately the protesters and naysayers were quieted or ignored and the line was built.

While highly specialized colliery railways using animal power had existed for more than a century and steam locomotives had been in limited use for more than a decade, the Stockton & Darlington was the first public railway to embrace the locomotive as a source of power. (The Surrey

Opening
Stockton & Darlington R.R.
1825

Iron Railway, built many years before the Stockton & Darlington, is often cited as the first public railway, but this line did not use steam locomotives.) Many people were highly skeptical of the new railway. Would it work? Were locomotives too dangerous to run in public? What if the engine were to fall off the tracks?

The Stockton & Darlington—often known as the Quaker Line because of the large role members of the Quaker religious sect played in financing it—was built by the visionary George Stephenson. Stephenson was a large, bony man, unusually strong and industrious. He had grown up in the north of England and had worked for a number of colliery lines in his youth. At the time of the Stockton & Darlington's charter, Stephenson was the most talented and experienced railway engineer in the world. While he did not invent either the steam locomotive or the railway, his brilliant vision largely shaped formative railway development in Britain. And in the early years of railway development British railway practice was the most influential in the world.

Stephenson played a fundamental role in the building of the Stockton & Darlington. He surveyed the line, engineered the railway, hired many of the laborers, and most importantly, suggested the use of steam locomotives instead of horses to haul its trains. While steam locomotives,

ABOVE: After pioneering the Stockton & Darlington, George Stephenson went on to engineer the more substantial Liverpool & Manchester Railway, whose completion on September 15, 1830, was celebrated in grand style.
OPPOSITE: Despite enormous skepticism and opposition, the multitalented Stephenson managed to build the world's first public railways, thanks to his combination of tremendous engineering skills and political savvy.

including some of Stephenson's own inventions, had been used on private coal-hauling lines, using steam locomotives on a public line was unprecedented. Yet his recommendation was accepted.

So, on that fateful September morning, after years of debate, struggle, and toil, Stockton & Darlington's first steam train was ready to roll. Stephenson had awaited this day with tremendous anticipation. It was the climax of his career. If anything went seriously wrong, the naysayers would have their day and it could doom future public railway ventures and ruin his reputation. If all went well, the steam locomotive could change the world! As thousands of spectators watched, Stephenson's locomotive, aptly named *Locomotion* and piloted by its builder, hauled some thirty-eight carriages, including the world's first railway passenger coach—an eighteen-seat vehicle named *Experiment*. Hundreds of exuberant passengers piled on board. In addition to the passenger carriage, there were a number of coal wagons. A pilot riding a horse preceded the train as it chugged triumphantly out of town. History was made.

Within a few years of the inauguration of the Stockton & Darlington, Stephenson had completed another, even more significant railway, the Liverpool & Manchester. By the early 1830s several lines were underway. As railway fever gripped England, across the Atlantic, in America, railways were also taking hold. Stephenson's son, Robert, a talented engineer in his own right, became one of the leading producers of locomotives in England. Perhaps no name is more closely associated with the pioneer days of railroading than Stephenson. They helped change the way the world moves.

Today, George Stephenson's portrait is featured on the British five-pound note.

The Chief, the Railroad, and the Priest

The Canadian Pacific was more than just another railroad; it was a patriotic endeavor designed to span Canada coast to coast and help unify the newly formed Dominion of Canada, which had officially come into being on July 15, 1867. Building the railroad was an epic undertaking, and the Canadian Pacific had to overcome numerous obstacles on its way west, from massive geological formations such as the Selkirk Mountains and Canadian Rockies to fearsome human resistance. Native Canadians—people often referred to as "Indians" at the time the railroad was being built— viewed the railroad as a hostile intrusion into their territory. In *The Last Spike*, a book about the building of the Canadian Pacific, author Pierre Burton tells a fascinating story of the impasse between the Blackfoot tribe and the railroad.

The Blackfoot resided on the open plains of western Canada near Calgary. Their leader, the great Crowfoot, was a man of mythic reputation. A warrior with nineteen battles behind him, he was an intelligent, proud, and handsome man, noted for his dignity, selfless bravery, and supreme fore-sight. Among his best-remembered deeds was his single-handed rescue of a helpless child from the grip of a grizzly bear—a beast that can rend a man limb from limb in seconds.

Crowfoot watched with dismay as the white men advanced westward into Blackfoot territory. Although a warrior, he first chose a peaceful resolution—in the late 1870s, prior to the advent of the Canadian Pacific, he signed a treaty with the Canadian government that essentially guaranteed the tribe a large tract of land. Crowfoot hoped this treaty would ensure the Blackfoot a secure future.

He was outraged, when, a few years later, railroad construction crews arrived near Blackfoot territory. He saw this as a breach of trust and a blatant incursion into Blackfoot land. Rather than attacking the builders immediately, he sent them a terse warning: if the railroad workers did not cease, he would dispatch seven hundred armed warriors to fight them. However, his warning went

OPPOSITE: The original railways met great resistance, but a generation later, tracks were being laid around the world. This train may look antique today, but it was the epitome of modern technology in its time, around the 1880s.

First recorded Canadian Pacific display advertisement, date June 28, 1886.

unheeded, and Crowfoot had nearly run out of practical alternatives. He was ready to launch a massacre when the one man who could prevent slaughter intervened. This was the missionary priest Albert Lacombe, who had the means to negotiate a settlement, but only if he had time to communicate effectively.

Lacombe was an amazingly unselfish man. He had developed a long and fruitful relationship with the Blackfoot and in years past had lived with them and helped them overcome adversity. In times of disease he had cared for their sick. In all likelihood there was no white man the Blackfoot held in higher regard than Lacombe. They trusted him like one of their own. Additionally, Lacombe had powerful connections among those of his own race.

Upon hearing of the impasse and knowing full well Crowfoot's position, Lacombe rode across the plains on horseback in an attempt to head off the railroad workers. Unfortunately, he was no more persuasive than the Blackfoot's own messengers. At the railroad camp he encountered a potentially fatal combination of ignorance, cynicism, and single-mindedness: the railroad was going to be built, and to hell with the Indians! Not one to waste time trying to persuade bone-headed railroad workers—who, if they had proceeded their way, would have ended up with their throats slit— Lacombe played his trump card. Years earlier he had impressed and befriended William Van Horne, Canadian Pacific's general manager, a man of considerable influence. Lacombe wired Van Horne, as well as other top Canadian Pacific officials, explaining the nature of the impasse and the likely outcome if the present course were not quickly altered. Van Horne had great respect for Lacombe, and he immediately recognized the seriousness of the situation. He ordered a halt to all construction, and asked Lacombe to negotiate a settlement with Crowfoot.

Lacombe approached the Blackfoot with gifts from Canadian Pacific—flour, sugar, tobacco, and tea—and asked for an audience with Chief Crowfoot and his council. It was granted, and Lacombe explained, in their language, that the white men were not trying to steal Blackfoot land, and that the men working out on the plain were just following the orders of their chiefs. The Blackfoot did not like what Lacombe had to say, but they trusted him and they listened. Lacombe continued by assuring them that if they restrained from attacking the railroad workers, he would bring the white men's "chief" to them so that they might work out an amicable settlement. Chief Crowfoot calmed his warriors, and announced that they would heed Lacombe's words. He knew that all his warriors could not prevent the railroad from being built, and that trying to stop the railroad would only result in gratuitous killing on both sides. If they could reach an honorable agreement in another way, so be it.

Later Edgar Dewdney, Lieutenant Governor of the Northwest Territories, met with Crowfoot and deeded more land to the Blackfoot as compensation for that taken to build the railway. One more hurdle had been cleared and many lives saved.

OPPOSITE: Unlike the American "transcon" of the 1860s, which despite its name ran only from California to Iowa, the Canadian Pacific Railway was a true transcontinental railroad—North America's first. RIGHT: Nineteenth-century railway building was a back-breaking business requiring thousands of men. A Canadian Pacific track gang labors away in the Lower Fraser Valley of British Columbia in 1883.

POWER RIVETING IN THE BOILER SHOP.

FORCING THE DRIVING WHEELS ON THEIR AXLES.

Selling Baldwin's Best

In the golden age of railroads, from the late nineteenth to the early twentieth century, new locomotives were one of the most valuable and sought-after commodities, especially in developing nations, such as those in eastern Europe, South America, and Asia. The locomotive was the key to industrial power and the symbol of a modern, progressive society. A nation was often judged by the condition of its railways and the status of its locomotives.

Samuel M. Vauclain, a longtime employee of the Baldwin Locomotive Works—the largest producer of locomotives in the world—worked his way up through the ranks, eventually assuming the role of company president and chairman of the board. A dapper gentleman, often sporting a bow tie and bowler hat, Vauclain was a brilliant salesman and a skilled promotion artist. He never missed an opportunity to sell his locomotives, and even as the company's highest officer he would often make personal visits to railroad presidents and heads of state in order to obtain orders for Baldwin's best. His autobiography, *Steaming Up!*, is filled with recollections, stories, and anecdotes of his experience selling locomotives.

Shortly after the end of World War I, Vauclain seized the opportunity to increase Baldwin's locomotive export business and traveled to eastern Europe to secure orders. Doing business there had special considerations. Vauclain relates:

My object in visiting Roumania [sic] was to sell the government a hundred locomotives. The market was almost feverishly active because most of the local motive power stood in yards or roundhouses marked, 'waiting for repairs,' or something like that. I wanted to sell, if I could be sure of payment. To the Minister of Public Works I explained, 'We cannot accept

OPPOSITE: For much of its early history, the locomotive was considered the pinnacle of mankind's technological achievements. Still, it took an awful lot of manual labor to bring a locomotive to life, as these engravings show.

Roumainian Treasury Bonds or Notes without something more substantial backing them than a promise to pay. There must be some merchantable collateral.'

'Roumania cannot go forward commercially unless it has locomotives,' he confessed. 'But it has neither money nor credit.'

Vauclain suggested that the country use its vast oil reserves as security. The idea was discussed among Romania's ministers and in short order Vauclain was meeting with the Romanian sovereign, King Ferdinand.

A jolly good fellow he proved to be. When I met him in his palace, to which he had invited me, I found him conversant with English as well as with conditions and needs of his country. 'Roumania must first build up its export trade,' he told me, 'before she can hope to pay her debts. Her most essential need is locomotives.'

We got along swimmingly.

Queen Marie, who later summoned me, was equally gracious and just as much alive to Roumania's need for locomotives. Our party lunched with the King and Queen. I was honored with a seat at the left of Her Majesty, who chatted freely and charmingly. Mind you, I was merely selling locomotives. After the luncheon and a brief visit in the Royal gardens during which Her Majesty submitted to having a photograph taken with me, my party adjourned to a business meeting with most of the Roumanian ministry.

ABOVE: The Romanian royal family was devoted to railways. Queen Marie was a friend of the Hill family, who built the Great Northern and other railways in the Pacific Northwest. Prince Nichols poses here in the cab of a Canadian locomotive.

Vauclain succeeded in securing a handsome order from Romania, on terms he found favorable. So important were his machines that he was treated with the respect of a foreign dignitary not only in Romania, but in other nations as well. Vauclain was immensely proud that his locomotives were used by nations around the world and were considered to be among the best.

Up in the Air

The highest railways in the world are located in South America, where rails crest more than two dozen summits over 10,000 feet (3048m) above sea level. The very highest lines are Central Railway of Peru's standard gauge lines: its highest through route reaches 15,694 feet (4784m) at the Galera Tunnel; however, its highest rail line is a branch to the Volcán Mine, which attains 15,806 feet (4818m) at La Cima. Another branch once reached even higher, to 15,848 feet (4830m), but it has been abandoned. In Brazil, the meter-gauge (a narrow gauge just one meter [3.3 ft] wide) Potosi Branch reaches 15,705 feet (4787m).

RIGHT: South American railways climb to dizzying heights. The highest lines in North America rarely exceed 11,000 feet (3353 m) above sea level, but this Peruvian train hauls copper to the lofty elevation of more than 15,000 feet (4572 m).

The Birthday Tunnel

Isambard Kingdom Brunel (1806–1859), the first chief engineer of Britain's Great Western Railway, was a visionary railroad designer who insisted on building the Great Western route from London to Bristol his own way. In general, he abhorred steep grades, and went out of his way to make sure the railroad was built with easy ones, with one notable exception. He created a steep tunnel through Box Hill in the Cotswolds, 96 miles (153km) west of London. Rather than climb the ridge and descend the far side at a low grade for 7 or 8 miles (11 or 13km), the GWR circled to the south and tunneled deep under Box Hill at a steep slope, reaching the floor of the next valley in just 2 miles (3.2km). The steep tunnel terrified passengers in the early days, who rode through it in the dark for twenty minutes.

This extreme bit of engineering was inconsistent with Brunel's often-expressed theories and was far more costly than the alternatives, but it can be explained by the vanity and showmanship of the brilliant engineer himself. Each year, on the anniversary of Brunel's birth, the sun shines through the tunnel from end to end. Accomplishment of this feat required a slope to match the angle of the sun's rays on that day.

ABOVE: Rising over Tennessee Pass, Colorado, the autumn sun gleams through the Deen Tunnel on the Denver & Rio Grande Western, illuminating nearby aspens.

Plane to the Train

The Québec Cartier Mining Company, the largest producer of iron ore in North America, operates a 240-mile (384km) railroad line between its mine at Mount Wright and Port Cartier, Québec. This line was built in the late 1950s for the primary purpose of moving ore, and it is entirely isolated from other railroad operations. It rises to an elevation of more than 2,000 feet (610m) above sea level and traverses the Canadian Shield, a horseshoe-shaped plateau, passing through some of the most remote wilderness in North America. In the more secluded areas the company must use helicopters to reach its trains in order to do routine maintenance, change crews, and help in an emergency.

RIGHT: The grand days of the luxury limiteds are long gone; nowadays North American railways serve primarily as freight-hauling lines. The Québec Cartier line, for example, is a virtual conveyor belt for iron ore.

Balloon Stack

In the early days of American railroading, wood-burning locomotives were equipped with elaborate smokestacks to prevent burning embers from starting fires and to direct smoke away from the train. The balloon stack was among the most popular and best known of these stacks and has come to typify locomotives from the period.

RIGHT: *The classic romantic image of a steam locomotive is a gleaming train with a mighty balloon stack.*

The Little Red Caboose

The first recorded use of a caboose was in the 1840s on the Auburn & Syracuse, a short line absorbed by the New York Central. Conductor Nat Wilson carried out his business while sitting on a wooden box at an upended barrel in an old boxcar that was tacked on to the end of a mixed freight-passenger train, and that contained his tools, chains, lanterns, and flares. Later, a caboose was placed at the rear of freight trains to provide shelter for railroaders working at that end and office space for the conductor.

The earliest known use of the word *caboose*, in 1855, was in reference to the conductors' cars on the Buffalo, Corning & New York. While cabooses were painted a variety of colors on different railroads, red was the most common for safety reasons. The "little red caboose" became one of the best-known aspects of traditional railroading. Cabooses had a host colorful monikers, being called everything from an angel's seat to a Waycar. A caboose was also known as a crummy.

However, evolving railroad technology and changes in railroad labor regulations eliminated the need for cabooses on most trains in the United States in the mid-1980s. They are still used occasionally in Canada, and can be found in regular use in Latin America.

RIGHT: Sadly, the wooden red caboose has largely faded into history. Cabooses still see occasional service on some lines, but in a more modern, less romantic incarnation—and they're not always that characteristic red.

The Cupola

Early cabooses lacked the distinctive, charming identifier of later cabooses: the cupola, whose invention is credited to conductor T. B. Watson of the Chicago & North Western.

According to a widely accepted story, Watson's regular, flat-topped caboose had been temporarily assigned to a work train, so an old boxcar was tacked onto the rear of his Cedar Rapids-to-Clinton freight train one sunny Iowa summer day in 1863. The car had a large hole in the roof, and Watson piled up some boxes and sat on top of them with his head and shoulders projecting above the roof. From this precarious perch he was able to watch the passing parade of grazing cattle and farmers at work in their fields, wave at pretty girls, and, incidentally, keep a watchful eye on the train rattling along ahead. Realizing the benefit of this "crow's nest," he reportedly sought out the C&NW master mechanic in Clinton, where two new cabooses were under construction, and suggested the "look-out" be included. The official agreed, and the C&NW became the first railroad to operate cabooses built with cupolas.

OPPOSITE: *Relics of another time, cabooses are more often found today away from the tracks, converted into restaurants or motels.*

The Caboose

From an old folk song:

Oh, the brakewheel's old and rusty, the shoes are thin and worn,

And she's loaded down with link and pin and chain,

And there's danger all around us as we try to pound our ear

In the little red caboose behind the train.

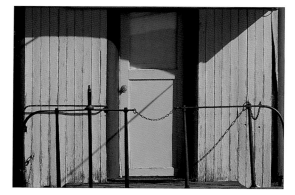

RIGHT: The caboose is one of the most enduring symbols of a bygone era of American railroading. Cabooses once brought up the rear on freight trains everywhere, bobbing along behind the tonnage that paid the bills. OPPOSITE: Watching the scenery glide past from the back of a caboose evokes glorious notions of freedom, but riding at the end of a freight train could be dangerous work.

The Pest in Pennsy's Offices

Raymond Loewy (1893–1986) may well be the best-known nonrailroader in the railroad world. He has left his mark on almost every area of product design, from postage stamps to NASA's Skylab, and has been credited with helping to pioneer the profession of industrial design. From a very young age, he was obsessed with transportation designs.

Loewy made himself such a pest in the offices of the mighty Pennsylvania Railroad that officials gave him the assignment of redesigning the trash cans in New York's Pennsylvania Station, just so they could get rid of him. He did such an outstanding job with the trash cans that he was invited to submit a proposal for the styling of the newly engineered GG1 locomtive.

His presentation of a clay model and some renderings shocked the Pennsy staff, since welding the entire shell was an automotive building technique, and not indigenous to the railroads. But Loewy's combination of a sleek streamlined body and an elegant five-strip "cat whisker" paint scheme of gold on Brunswick green carried the day, resulting in one of the truly great locomotive designs.

Loewy's relationship with the Pennsylvania Railroad Company went on for many years. He ultimately moved on to designs for ships, the Studebaker Avanti, Air Force One and other aircraft, and NASA products.

OPPOSITE: The GG1 electric locomotive was one of the most famous trains of the twentieth century. Its revolutionary streamlined design was dreamt up by industrial designer Raymond Loewy. ABOVE: One of the world's mightiest corporations at the turn of the twentieth century, the Pennsylvania Railroad wasn't just a railroad—it was an empire.

Chapter Two

ENGINES THAT COULD

FAMOUS TRAINS

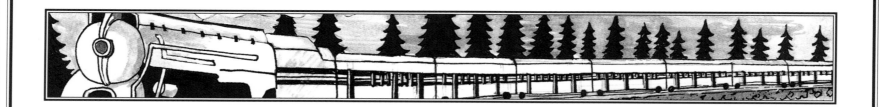

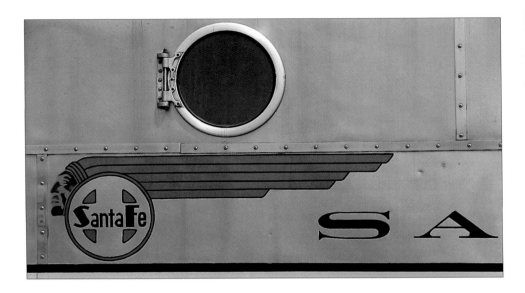

For more than a century the sight of a train has inspired children and adults, men and women, poets and artists, technicians and technologists. Who can deny the romance and power of a passing train?

Railways took special pride in their first-class limiteds and high-speed expresses. These trains were assigned the finest equipment, given colorful, distinctive names, and advertised with pride and enthusiasm. Some trains are legendary: New York Central ran the *Empire State Express* and *Twentieth Century Limited*; Santa Fe operated its *Chief*, *Super Chief*, and *El Capitan*; Illinois Central had its famous *City of New Orleans*; and Baltimore & Ohio (known to Monopoly players by its initials, "B&O") had its *Capitol Limited* and *Royal Blue*. Lesser-known lines had their famous trains too. One of the best-known trains in the United States in the early twentieth century was the Lackawanna's *Phoebe Snow*.

Other trains were known worldwide for their exotic routing or the astounding scenery they traversed. The *Orient Express* traveled over dramatic territory and vast steppes, connecting the grand cities of Europe with gateways to the cities of Asia and the Far East. Canadian Pacific's fabulous *Canadian* was noted for its crossing of the spectacular Canadian Rockies. For generations, these trains and many others have been the settings for true tales and the inspiration for fictional ones.

PAGE 37: *The Delaware, Lackawanna & Western's* Lackawanna *is wreathed in its own steam as it prepares to depart the station.* OPPOSITE: *Railway travel at its very best was epitomized by New York Central's renowned* Twentieth Century Limited, *a luxury, all-Pullman sleeper train that ran at top speeds between New York and Chicago.* ABOVE: *Atchison, Topeka & Santa Fe, which connected the Midwest with Texas and California, utilized a southwestern motif in their company imagery, as well as a famous slogan, "Santa Fe all the way."*

Puffing Billy

In 1813, Christopher Blackett and William Hedley built a steam locomotive combining the best

features of several earlier designs. It was one of the earliest locomotives to have the steam exhaust-

ed through the smokestack, increasing the draft for the fire and creating a pronounced "chuffing"

noise, thus earning the nickname Puffing Billy.

OPPOSITE: *In a scene repeated*
thousands of times all across America
during the glory days of railroading,
a steam locomotive rolls through a
snowy landscape on a crisp February
afternoon. RIGHT: The image of the
steam locomotive puffing through end-
less unspoiled landscape symbolized
man's ability to conquer nature: no
place was too remote, too wild, or too
rugged for the train.

The Fastest Train in the World

Commodore Vanderbilt's New York Central & Hudson River Railroad, a line that connected New York City with Chicago, pioneered high-speed train service. The very definition of "high speed" has changed over the past century and a half. In the 1820s, railroad pioneer George Stephenson argued for trains that would run at 12 to 15 mph (19.2–24kph), a speed considered dangerously fast by some at the time. Today, trains in Europe and Japan regularly operate at speeds up to 180 mph (288kph). But in the last quarter of the nineteenth century, any train that ran in excess of 60 mph (96kph) was considered fast, and the railroad was then pushing the envelope of land speed. "Faster than a speeding locomotive" was a phrase that captured the imaginations of children and challenged the skills of locomotive engineers.

On September 14, 1891, New York Central inaugurated a new train called the *Empire State Express*. This glamorous passenger train redefined the term *express*. Known popularly as the "Fastest Train in the World," it operated at an average speed of 61.4 mph (98.2kph), including station stops. With this high-speed train, the railroad's general passenger agent, George Henry Daniels, whom railroad writer Lucius Beebe described as "one of the great railroad promotion men of all time," masterminded a stunt that would capture the world's attention. In cooperation with the Schenectady Locomotive Works, New York Central's motive power chief, William Buchanan, built a locomotive designed to run faster than any other ever had before. This special locomotive, No. 999, designed for high-speed service, was an outstanding machine with driving wheels (the wheels that move the locomotive, as opposed to running wheels, which carry it) seven feet (2.1 m) tall. The larger the driving wheels, the greater the speed of the train. No. 999 was assigned to the *Empire State Express* especially to whisk passengers from New York City to Chicago for the

OPPOSITE: The fastest thing on steel wheels in the 1890s, New York Central's famed Empire State Express *zips along, the locomotive's throttle opened wide. ABOVE: Schenectady Locomotive Works helped create the world's fastest train in the early 1890s. This locomotive builder's plate comes from one of their later products.*

Columbian Exposition—a magnificent fair heralding the four hundredth anniversary of Columbus's arrival in the New World.

On May 10, 1893, the Chicago-bound *Empire State Express* rolled into Syracuse, New York, a little behind schedule. At Syracuse, locomotive No. 999, under the throttle of veteran engineer Charles M. Hogan, was linked to the *Express*. Hogan was an exceptionally capable locomotive engineer, well known for his skill.

Some of the railroad's top brass boarded the train—they had planned an extraordinary run and did not want to miss it. The *Empire State Express* rolled out of Syracuse and on toward Buffalo. On the way to Buffalo, between Rochester and the village of Batavia, the railroad climbs a short but noteworthy grade. West of Batavia the tracks follow one of the longest tangent level sections on the New York Central—a line popularly known as the Water Level Route for its nearly gradeless profile. It was here that engineer Hogan, already moving along at a good speed, adjusted No. 999's valves for the fastest speed possible and opened the throttle as wide as it would go. The *Empire State Express* raced toward Buffalo faster than any train had ever moved. It clipped away a mile (1.6km) in just 36 seconds, for a speed of 112 mph (179kph)! Hogan set the world speed record, a superlative that remained on the books for more than a dozen years. Newspapers around the world carried the story of engineer Hogan and the No. 999.

For many years that fast locomotive was the most famous ever to run, although some now claim that the speed record was invalid because of improper timing methods. Today, locomotive No. 999 is displayed proudly at the Chicago Museum of Science. To contemporary viewers it probably seems like an antique, but it was once the fastest machine in the world. The railroad between Batavia and Buffalo is still a busy route, although more than a hundred years after No. 999's exemplary performance, passenger trains on this stretch of track are restricted by federal law to just 79 mph (126kph)!

OPPOSITE: Long trips became even longer when water and fuel stops caused delays. To speed things along, New York Central employed a network of water pans between the rails that allowed locomotives to fill their tenders without stopping.

Phoebe Snow

Romantic visions of turn-of-the-century train travel are rarely hampered by the real-life concerns of soot and cinders. However, in the days when coal-burning locomotives hauled trains, passengers expected to arrive at their destination covered by a grimy film of soot.

Promoters of the Delaware, Lackawanna & Western, a line that connected Hoboken, New Jersey—directly across the Hudson River from New York City—and Buffalo, New York, found a way to distinguish their service from their competition. A half dozen routes connected the New York City area and the "Queen City," and while Lackawanna's was not the fastest, the shortest, nor the cheapest, it was the cleanest. Rather than burning soft, sooty bituminous coal in its locomotives, the Lackawanna burned hard, clean anthracite coal—a commodity that also, not coincidentally, represented a fair amount of the company's lucrative freight traffic. So beginning in 1900, the Lackawanna launched a vigorous advertising campaign designed to attract passengers and simultaneously promote anthracite coal.

The man in blue
Now helps her through,
And tells her when
Her train is due.
"He's so polite.
They do things right
Upon the Road
of
Anthracite"

Lackawanna Railroad

The willing porter
Doth escort her

This is the Road of Anthracite

ABOVE & OPPOSITE: Maintaining a clean white dress aboard a typical steam-powered passenger train was a laughable proposal on most railroads, which burned sooty bituminous coal. But Lackawanna assured passengers an unsullied ride thanks to the use of clean-burning anthracite.

Lackawanna's premier train was named the *Phoebe Snow*, after a fictional female passenger purported to ride the line. Phoebe was a striking woman, known for her good taste, snow white gown, pleasant smile, and porcelain complexion. Her costume for her train journey was considered extraordinary because under normal circumstances no sane woman would have worn a white dress on a long train trip—and that was precisely Lackawanna's gimmick!

Phoebe was featured in a long-running series of illustrated newspaper and magazine ads. Her likeness was used on railroad promotional literature and timetables. Each ad also featured a different, but rhymed ditty. Over the years dozens of different verses were composed, such as:

A cosey seat
A dainty treat
Make Phoebe's
Happiness complete
With linen white
And silver bright
Upon the Road
Of Anthracite.

Lackawanna Railroad

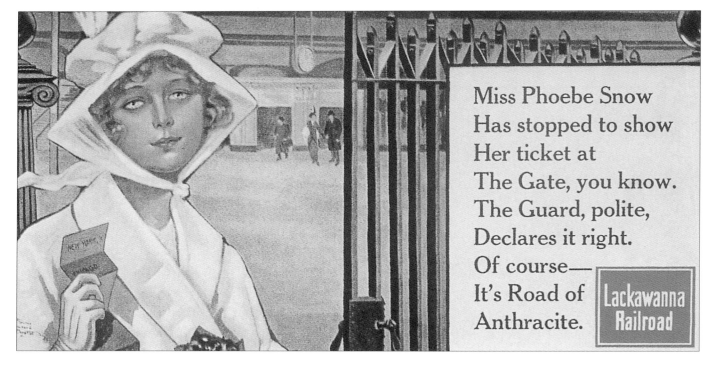

Miss Phoebe Snow
Has stopped to show
Her ticket at
The Gate, you know.
The Guard, polite,
Declares it right.
Of course—
It's Road of
Anthracite.

Lackawanna Railroad

> It's time to go
> With Phoebe Snow
> Where banks of rhododendron blow.

> In pink and white
> On every height
> Along the Road of Anthracite

The themes varied a bit, but most revolved around the cleanliness of the line and its use of anthracite coal.

> Here is the maiden all in lawn
> Who boarded the train one early morn
> That runs on the Road of Anthracite,

> And when she left the train that night
> She found, to her surprised delight
> Hard coal had kept her dress still bright.

Many of the ditties, particularly the later ones, used a fixed seven-line format and an established rhyme scheme. By far the most famous and most often repeated of all the slogans was:

> Says Phoebe Snow
> About to go
> Upon a trip
> To Buffalo,

> "My gown stays white
> From morn till night
> Upon the Road of Anthracite."

The campaign was enormously successful, and by 1910, Phoebe Snow was among the most famous women in the United States. Many folks didn't realize she was merely a fictional persona, and she was so popular she often received gifts from satisfied passengers. Also, it is said, she received a fair number of marriage proposals from eligible bachelors.

Lackawanna ran the *Phoebe Snow* for 60 years; the line was known simply as the "Route of the Phoebe Snow." In 1960, the *Phoebe Snow* was discontinued for a few years, but it was later revived. However, by the late 1960s, demand for first-class passenger service had diminished and the train was again discontinued, this time for good. Yet, the legend of Phoebe Snow lives on in the annals of advertising and railroad lore.

OPPOSITE: Lackawanna built its ingenious advertising campaign around its boast of a clean ride and embodied the concept through a series of jingles about the mythical Phoebe Snow, an attractive, pristinely attired woman who symbolized the company's most prestigious train.

Robbery on the Orient Express

Introduced in 1883, the *Orient Express* set the standard for elegant train travel. The train, whose route spanned the European continent, provided luxurious surroundings for wealthy passengers, in addition to an exotic setting for novels and movies. The first *Orient Express* included three coaches, with partitions carved and inlaid using teak, walnut, and mahogany; silk bedsheets; gold plumbing fixtures; and marble sinks. An elegant car that included a men's smoking compartment, a library, and a ladies' lounge followed the coaches, but the dining car was the most opulent. Carved wood was a sumptuous background to crystal chandeliers and paintings; linen-covered tables were adorned with fine china, sterling silver, and crystal. It was common for the aristocratic passengers to dine in full evening dress and to be entertained with live music. The *Orient Express* came to symbolize mystery and intrigue, opulence and luxury.

In his book *Orient Express*, British journalist E.H. Cookridge tells of the great robbery on this famous train. On May 31, 1891, in a thickly forested region of Turkey, twenty or so armed bandits waited near the tracks that carried the *Orient Express*. Today these men would be labeled terrorists—although in those days there was no such word—because they were not out for personal gain so much as to further their political agenda. The robbers had sabotaged the tracks with the intent to derail and rob the train. In the 1880s and 1890s train robbery had become an almost common activity among petty thieves, but these men were rebels of a sort, led by a large man known just as Anasthatos, who had a thick black beard. The region of Turkey the train traveled through was fraught with political strife.

The westbound *Orient Express* came upon the section of sabotaged track. The engineer attempted to stop the train but there was no time. The train derailed and the locomotive and first couple of cars toppled into the ditch. The last cars, those carrying high-paying first-class passen-

OPPOSITE: Over its long life the Orient Express *used many routes and many different railways. Here, shortly before World War I, the renowned train crosses a distinctly European landscape.*

gers, remained upright and undamaged. The *Orient Express* had not been moving particularly fast, and no one was killed in the crash, although a number of people were banged up and greatly frightened by the abrupt stop and subsequent tumbling. During the first moments of chaos, Anasthatos and his gang, brandishing their weapons, rounded up the train crew and passengers as they escaped from the wreckage. Women shrieked and men panicked as the fearsome bandits did their work, but Anasthatos hollered for passengers to remain calm. He assured them that no one would be killed if they cooperated with him. The train crew were bound hand and foot and forced to lie on the ground, while the passengers were systematically robbed of their money and valuables.

When a man struggled with one of the bandits he was shot in the arm. This outburst angered Anasthatos, who struck down the offending member of his gang. Probably realizing that such brutality against his victims would hurt his cause and damage his reputation, he personally attended to the wounded man, apologizing for the injury. This did not prevent the bandits from continuing with their heist, and all told they stole thousands of dollars worth of gold, gems, and currency. Furthermore, Anasthatos identified several wealthy German businessmen riding in the first-class compartments and took them as hostages. Soon the bandits had fled the scene with them.

Eventually a rescue train was dispatched to pick up the remaining passengers. Turkish authorities pursued the bandits without results. Anasthatos demanded a healthy ransom for the Germans, and the kidnapping nearly resulted in hostilities between Germany and Turkey. The Turkish authorities were helpless to apprehend Anasthatos, and any attempt at rescue might have resulted in the death of the hostages. Ultimately, Anasthatos got his ransom, and he released the Germans physically unharmed, each with a gold coin as a gift from him for their trouble. The *Orient Express* resumed service, but Anasthatos remained at large—he and his bandits were never caught.

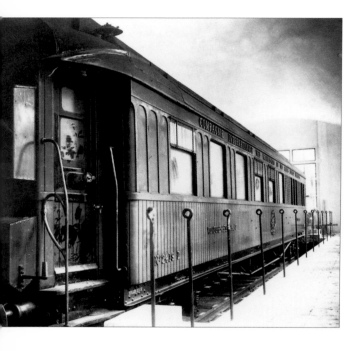

ABOVE: *The* Orient Express *carried well-to-do passengers in the most luxurious carriages, but it was not simply the furnishings that lent this famous train its indelible magic; it was the mystique of journeying through exotic lands.*

The Ghan

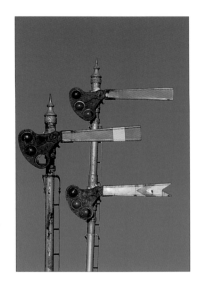

The *Ghan*, which carries passengers and freight over the Trans-Australian Railway, is one of the few mixed-use trains in the world with a formal name. Serving the isolated interior of Australia, it crosses the great Victoria Desert from Adelaide, passes the Musgrave and Macdonnell Ranges, and reaches many cut-off communities, following the path of the Afghan-camel drivers for which it was named. The *Ghan* ran once a week until the 1970s, but from 1990 to the present, a second train has been put into use from May to October.

ABOVE: If signaling devices can be considered visually appealing, lower quadrant semaphores are probably the most aesthetically pleasing. Though weathered and worn, these signals have faithfully protected American railways for nearly one hundred years. RIGHT: A yard limit sign near Golden, Colorado, attracts a curious crow.

The Longest Railway

Russia's Trans-Siberian Railway is the longest unbroken railway line in the world. It runs more than 6,000 miles (9600km) and spans western Russia from the Urals—the range of mountains that acts as a boundary between Asia and Europe—to the Pacific port of Vladivostok, situated on the Sea of Japan. This great railway serves as the sole means of access to much of Siberia, an extremely remote area known for its exceptional harshness, vast size, and those unfortunate people exiled to it. Much of the railway was built using convict laborers during Tsarist times, prior to the Russian Revolution of 1917. Like many of those living in this region, the railroad builders were not there of their own choice. After the railroad was completed, it was used to transport tens of thousands of Russian exiles to this isolated region, especially following the revolution.

In modern times the ride across the Trans-Siberian from Moscow to Vladivostok takes 10 to 12 days, as the train rarely moves much faster than 30 miles per hour (48kph). However, in its early days, the Trans-Siberian was even more notorious for its poor engineering, shoddy construction, and bad track. Far from the scrutiny of Moscow, operations on the line were conducted in a haphazard fashion. Compared to the punctuality of other railroads of the time, the Trans-Siberian was a real horror. In the book *To the Great Ocean*, author Harmon Tupper relates a story told by Robert L. Jefferson, who rode the line its early days:

ABOVE: Thousands of miles from Moscow, a train pauses near Novonnikolaevsk, Siberia. The name Siberia has become synonymous with the idea of a distant land, but the railroad made the steppes reachable.
OPPOSITE: It's a long but scenic route across the vast Western Siberian Lowlands and Central Siberian Plateau.

Bang out in the middle of the steppe, miles from anywhere, the train one day brought up suddenly, and stuck there for three hours . . . . None of our Russian passengers ventured to inquire the cause of the train's inertion [sic], neither did the conductor, who periodically passed through the train with the face about as intelligible as a sphinx, volunteer any information on the subject. [Thomas] Gaskell [Jefferson's traveling partner] and I, however, descended, walked along the line to the engine, and discovered that the tank had burst and the water was cheerfully washing away the track. The engineer was complacently leaning against the buffers smoking papiros [sic], his fireman was asleep in the cab of the tender, nobody else was about, and the whole situation was so sublime that, being in the condition to laugh at anything, we both laughed heartily.

OPPOSITE: The completion of the Trans-Siberian Railway facilitated the settlement of this exceptionally remote region. Between 1894 and 1914 nearly five million Russian peasants emigrated or were exiled to Siberia via the railway. RIGHT: Built by the Tsar, the Trans-Siberian Railway—the longest line in the world—was instrumental to the cohesion of the massive country.

Chapter Three

RIDING THAT TRAIN

TRAIN TRAVEL

The romance of train travel has lured passengers to the rails for some two centuries.

While early trains were far from luxurious, they offered a significantly faster mode of travel than anything that had ever been known before. As the railroads matured and railways enhanced their trains to successfully compete with each other for passengers, the quality of travel dramatically improved. No expense was spared to attract wealthy customers. Some train cars were among the most opulent vehicles ever to roll over land. In the golden age of railroading, between 1890 and about 1920, long-distance passenger trains featured luxurious coaches with elaborately cushioned chairs, deluxe sleeping cars with every modern amenity, fancy parlor cars with large windows for viewing scenery, and splendid dining cars with chefs capable of preparing everything from a simple snack to a gourmet meal.

Railways were known for their "flagship trains," fancy premier limiteds that demonstrated a railway company's prosperity. Many flagship trains were household names, and people dreamed of riding on them. The Pennsylvania Railroad had its famous *Broadway Limited*, Southern Pacific the legendary *Overland Limited*, Baltimore & Ohio the glamorous *Royal Blue*, and Canadian Pacific its signature *Canadian*. Just riding these trains conferred prestige and status upon passengers. There was simply no better way to go.

Even for those passengers who couldn't afford the steep fares of the luxury trains, riding the train offered excitement and adventure. Going somewhere—fast—as the scenery sped by, and dreaming of far-off places, could be the experience of a lifetime for anyone.

PAGE 59: The world's first diesel-powered articulated passenger train ushered in the era of streamlined steam in 1934. Soon a shining fleet of stainless-steel streamliners was connecting major cities of the midwestern United States on the Burlington Route. OPPOSITE: The Pennsylvania Railroad, the self-proclaimed "Standard Railroad of the World," welcomes passengers aboard its twenty-seventh anniversary Broadway Limited at Pennsylvania Station, New York. RIGHT: Southern Pacific's noted Sunset route gave passengers a look at the beautiful southwestern deserts between California and Texas. The Sunset Limited connected San Francisco to New Orleans by way of Los Angeles.

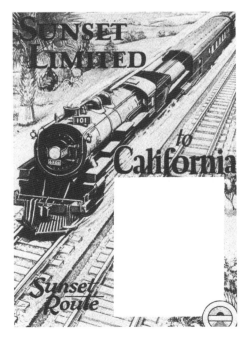

From a Railway Carriage

Faster than fairies, faster than witches,

Bridges and houses, hedges and ditches;

And charging along the troops in battle,

All through the meadows the horses and cattle.

—Robert Louis Stevenson

OPPOSITE: Steaming through a dreamy winter landscape, the famous Dreyfuss Hudson whisks passengers aboard New York Central's Twentieth Century Limited *between Chicago and New York. RIGHT: Few sights are as compelling as a puffing steam locomotive struggling against a rugged mountain landscape.*

I Like to See it Lap the Miles

The American poet Emily Dickinson wrote of the diminutive steam-hauled train that passed near her home in Amherst, Massachusetts:

> I like to see it lap the Miles—
> And lick the Valleys up—
> And stop to feed itself at Tanks—
> And then—prodigious step
>
> Around a Pile of Mountains—
> And supercilious peer
> In Shanties—by the side of roads—
> And then a quarry pare
>
> To fit its Ribs
> And crawl between
> Complaining all the while
> In horrid—hooting stanza—
> Then chase itself down Hill—
>
> And neigh like Boanerges—
> Then—punctual as a Star
> Stop—docile and omnipotent
> At its own stable door—

RIGHT: On a bright, Colorado morning, a Cumbres & Toltec locomotive pulls up to a water tank to fill its tender with water, in preparation for its arduous climb over the Rocky Mountains. OPPOSITE: An aged Baldwin locomotive rolls through the pastoral fields and mountain glens of central Pennsylvania. The passing steam train was once a common sight across rural North America.

The Pan American

song by Hank Williams

I've heard your stories about your fast trains

But now I'll tell you about one . . .

She's the Beauty of the Southland!

Listen to that whistle scream . . .

It's the Pan-American . . .

On her way to New Orleans!

RIGHT: *Once heard, the sound of a brass steam whistle echoing through a valley is not soon forgotten. Many loco-motives had distinctive whistles; some were high-pitched shrieks, others were long, mournful wails.*

The Beanery

A beanery was a railroader's eating place, so named because it was where he ate his beans. The beanery was often owned and operated by the railroad for its employees at an out-of-the-way location that might not otherwise warrant a restaurant. Waitresses at beaneries were called beanery queens. Many beanery queens married railroadmen. This was a function of the working conditions of the time. Railroad work, particularly in engine service, was considered fairly prestigious in the nineteenth century, and enginemen rarely had trouble supporting a household. However, because they often spent much of their time operating far away from the civilized population, they did not have many opportunities to meet eligible women. So beaneries served as matchmaking places as well as eateries.

RIGHT: In the American West, railways often served remote Podunks—tiny villages many miles from true civilization. To accommodate train crews, the railway provided cooks and kitchens.

Travel

Edna St. Vincent Millay

The railroad track is miles away

and the day is loud with voices speaking,

yet there isn't a train goes by all day

but I hear its whistle shrieking

All night there isn't a train goes by

though the night is still for sleeping and dreaming

but I see its cinders red on the sky

and hear its engine steaming

My heart is warm with the friends I make,

And better friends I'll not be knowing;

Yet there isn't a train I wouldn't take,

No matter where it's going

RIGHT: Craftsmanship and elegance were highly valued commodities in the age of wooden passenger cars. The cars were typically coated with many layers of varnish, and thus were known as "varnish" by railroaders to distinguish them from more ordinary freight cars. OPPOSITE: Like its better-known cousin, the Simplon Orient Express *passed through many exotic nations. Here the train pauses in Bulgaria on its run to Istanbul.*

Milk Run

Many North American railroads, particularly in New England, upstate New York, and the maritime provinces of Canada, operated mixed trains (those that carried both freight and passengers) that carried fresh milk in farming regions. Milk trains often featured special cars designed to keep the milk from spoiling and were typically operated ahead of passenger cars. While the milk trains were tightly scheduled, they usually made numerous lengthy stops to pick up milk canisters along the way and took much longer to make it over the same route than other trains did. Passengers in a hurry would usually avoid milk trains in favor of a faster train, usually one of the named "limiteds." After a while any local passenger train that made frequent stops came to be known as "the milk run," even if the train never carried anything but passengers.

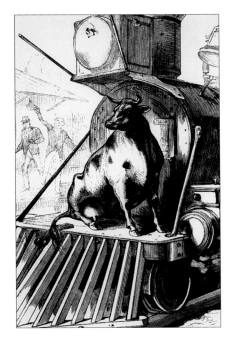

OPPOSITE: Ireland was one of the earliest nations to adopt the railway. A locomotive of the Dublin & South Eastern line (known affectionately as the Dirty, Slow & Easy) climbs northward toward the summit at Rathdrum. RIGHT: Since tracks in North America were rarely fenced in, locomotives were equipped with "cowcatchers" to keep stray livestock away—but this 1880s image offers another perspective!

The City of New Orleans

song by Steve Goodman

Ridin' on *The City of New Orleans*,

Illinois Central Monday morning rail,

Fifteen cars and fifteen restless riders,

three conductors, twenty-five sacks of mail.

All on the southbound odyssey

the train pulls out of Kankakee

and rolls past houses, farms and fields;

passing towns that had no name and

freight yards full of old black men and

the graveyards of rusted automobiles.

Singin' "Good morning America! How are you?

Say, don't you know me? I'm your native son.

I'm the train they call *The City of New Orleans*.

I'll be gone five hundred miles when day is done."

Dealin' card games with the old men in the club car.

Penny a point and no one's keeping score.

Pass the paper bag that holds the bottle

and feel the wheels a-rumblin' 'neath the floor.

And the sons of Pullman porters and the sons of engineers

ride their fathers' magic carpet made of steel.

OPPOSITE: Illinois Central jumped on the streamliner bandwagon in 1936, ordering a classy Pullman-built speedster called the Green Diamond *to whisk passengers between Chicago and St. Louis.*

And mothers with their babes asleep

are rocking to the gentle beat,

the rhythm of the rail is all they dream.

"Good morning America! How are you?

Say, don't you know me? I'm your native son.

I'm the train they call *The City of New Orleans*.

I'll be gone 500 miles when day is done."

Nighttime on *The City of New Orleans*,

changing cars in Memphis, Tennessee.

Halfway home and we'll be there by morning,

through the Mississippi darkness rollin' to the sea.

But all the towns and people seem to fade into a bad dream.

Well, the steel rail hasn't heard the news:

The conductor sings his song again

it's the "passengers will please refrain,

this train has the disappearin' railroad blues."

"Goodnight America! How are you?

Say, don't you know me? I'm your native son.

I'm the train they call *The City of New Orleans*.

I'll be gone 500 miles when day is done."

OPPOSITE: *A highly polished General Motors–built Illinois Central diesel symbolizes a hopeful new era in rail travel. In poignant contrast, the song* The City of New Orleans, *highlighting IC's most famous train, depicts the sad decline of North American train travel.*

Chapter Four

I've Been Working on the Railroad

Heroes and Heroines

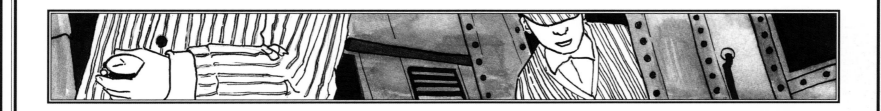

Working on the railway has more than its fair share of perils, and as a result men and women of the railroads have inspired innumerable tales of risk, heroism, and tragedy.

Locomotive engineers were often heroes to little boys growing up around the tracks. These men held the power of the engine in their hands. They could race down the track at great speed with famous limiteds in tow; or bring long, heavy trains up over the mountains, through long tunnels, and across towering trestles. These skilled, daring men were responsible for driving trains safely and swiftly across the land. Their locomotives were powerful and dangerous machines with state-of-the-art technology. There seemed to be no limit to the speed or power of a locomotive, and a clever throttle artist could manipulate the force of the engine to get just a little bit more out of it.

Yet every run brought the risk of accident and death. The locomotive engineer was a man with great responsibility who put his life on the line. A wrong move could result in an accident or explosion. A lapse of judgment or mechanical failure could be deadly. Some of those brave men met their glory with their hands on the throttle or gripped tightly to the brake handle, whatever the situation called for.

While enginemen are heralded as heroes, the lesser-known employees of the rails—brakemen, clerks, and telegraphers, along with Pullman porters, train dispatchers, and a host of others—ought not be forgotten. They too play a crucial role in the working of the railway, and many have grand tales to tell. Yet songwriters, storytellers, and poets are far more likely to glorify the engineer who perishes in a spectacular accident caused by his own neglect than the faithful baggage handler who performed his job with pride and excellence throughout his career. Here, we extol the everyday working men and women on the railroad.

PAGE 77: As steam locomotives became more powerful, their boilers had to get much larger. Here, some gargantuan boilers are shown in various stages of production in a huge train shed. OPPOSITE: For much of railroading's early history, the engineer was a heroic figure, a man with incredible forces at his command. ABOVE: By the 1940s, the diesel-electric was seen as a panacea for a railroad's woes. In this montage a diesel-electric's engineer rolls along on the mainline past a long steam-powered passenger train.

Casey Jones

Casey Jones was the most famous locomotive engineer ever to roll the American high iron. His name, shrouded in legend, is synonymous with the golden age of railroading.

A dashing, tall man with gray eyes and dark hair, Casey was a hero in his own time and his name became one to be remembered for all time. While the cause of his death might have been his own carelessness, he is remembered because he upheld the ideals of the time and sacrificed his own life to protect the lives of his crew and passengers.

He was born John Luther Jones on March 14, 1864, and lived in Cayce, Kentucky, for a time. He came to be known as "Cayce" Jones to distinguish him from the legions of other John Joneses. The spelling of his nickname was later changed to the more common Casey. He took a job with the railroad when he was sixteen and worked on the railway in one capacity or another for his whole career. In 1888, he hired on with the Illinois Central, a line that ran (and still runs) from Chicago to New Orleans by way of Memphis. A skilled, popular man, Casey quickly worked his way up through the ranks and was promoted to locomotive engineer in 1890. Soon he was in good company, as his three brothers all became Illinois Central engineers. Although he ran the locomotive, his first assignment was not glamorous. While more experienced men were working the throttles on fast passenger trains, Casey was learning the ropes working a lowly yard goat—a small engine used to sort railroad cars. He did his work well and in short order was promoted to service on the mainline. For a while he ran a train nicknamed the "Irish Mail."

In Casey's time, locomotive crews were often assigned a specific engine. They were responsible for the locomotive's appearance, performance, and general upkeep. If the engine developed a problem, it was the engineer's responsibility to report it to the mechanics in the roundhouse and see that it was fixed. A railroader took great pride in his locomotive and its performance. Many lines handed out

OPPOSITE: Casey Jones poses in the cab of Illinois Central 638, the locomotive he was regularly assigned in freight service. Had he remained a freight engineer, it's likely he would have enjoyed a long, productive life and languished happily in relative obscurity.

ABOVE: Casey Jones was a high roller who took chances, but his sincere dedication to the safety of passengers and crew made him a symbol of his profession, and transformed him into a folk hero, celebrated on a U.S. postage stamp.

bonuses to engineers who, through efficient operation, used less coal. For many years Casey was assigned to Illinois Central No. 638, a powerful 2-8-0 (referring to the wheel alignment) Consolidation type. This was a freight locomotive, so Casey regularly hauled the railroad's freight trains.

Many engineers were known by their distinctive whistles; Casey was no exception. He had his own special whistle: a melodic, six-chime calliope that he had mastered. When he rolled through the towns along the "IC," his whistle rang out its signature sound. It is said that it mimicked the sound of his name, and echoed "Kaaaaaaa Ceeeeee JOOooonessss" as he rolled along.

The railroad was run by a book of rules that dictated how and when trains were to move over the line. Everyone who operated trains was familiar with the rules, and there is an old adage that states: "There is a body behind every rule in the book." The rules were designed for safety, not for expediency, and some engineers stretched them when regulations threatened to slow them down. Casey was a maverick and high roller known for getting his trains over the railroad in good time. He was proud of his conservative use of coal and his abbreviated stops for water. When his engine needed a repair, small or large, he made sure the mechanics attended to it promptly.

However, with regard to the rules, Casey was less observant. During the course of ten years, he was called on the carpet nine times for negligence regarding regulations, and several times he was suspended from service for thirty days. Although he was involved in some minor accidents, he prided himself on never having killed or injured anyone while running his locomotive, and his skill for making his run in good time was appreciated by train dispatchers and others. They could always count on Casey to keep to the schedule and bring his train in on time.

Casey's fast running paid off; he was promoted to passenger service, and at the very turn of the century, on January 1, 1900, he began running IC's premier passenger train, the *New Orleans Special*, a train better known by its nickname, "The Cannonball." This was the fastest regularly scheduled train on the railroad, and to run it was a privilege. With this prestige came an ample raise.

For Casey, the one downside to this run was that he had to leave his favorite locomotive, old No. 638, behind. While an excellent freight hauler, No. 638 was not designed to haul fast passenger trains. For this job, Casey was assigned the high-drivered (referring to its tall driving wheels, which gave it great speed) ten-wheeler locomotive No. 382. One rainy night, a few months after his promotion, Casey and his fireman (the railroader responsible for maintaining the fire on a steam locomotive, who also acted as a second set of eyes)—an intelligent, soft-spoken black man named Sim Webb—arrived in Memphis on a northbound passenger train, only to find that the regular engineer scheduled on the southbound Cannonball was ill. The southbound train was running late into Memphis, so Casey and Sim agreed to take it south to Canton, Mississippi, when it arrived. Between runs they got a few hours sleep, and No. 382 was serviced and made ready for the run. When the Cannonball arrived in Memphis it was an hour and a half behind schedule. Casey took the train and agreed to make up the lost time. He said to Sim, "We're going to have a pretty tough time getting into Canton on the dot, but I believe we can do it, barring accidents."

ABOVE: The railroad fireman had the arduous but essential job of maintaining the fire in the boiler by shoveling tons of coal. On a heavy run a fireman might shovel half a ton of coal every hour.

They left Memphis in mist and rain and raced southward towards Canton. The engine was running well that night, and the run was on a long, straight track, so between Memphis and Sardis, Mississippi, Casey shortened his cutoff (adjusted the valves for fast running), opened his throttle, and raced along, clipping away a mile (1.6km) every fifty seconds. Between every station they made up time. Casey was confident he would pull into Canton on time. However, ahead of him at the town of Vaughan was a situation he had not counted on: two freights, one headed south and one north, simultaneously trying to squeeze into a passing siding to get "in the clear" (out of the way) of Casey's Cannonball. Unfortunately, the southbound train did not fit, and its last car and caboose were sticking out on the mainline. The freight conductor had gone back and put a warning torpedo—an explosive used to signal a train to stop—on the tracks.

Casey approached Vaughan not expecting traffic ahead. As his train leaned into the curve approaching the siding it crushed the torpedo left to warn him, but he never heard the sound and he continued along as fast as he dared. Moments later, Sim saw the lights of the southbound's caboose and he screamed across the cab to Casey at the top of his voice, "Look out, we're gonna hit something!"

Without turning his head, Casey shouted, "Jump, Sim!" as he frantically applied the brakes. Sim jumped and lived to tell the tale; Casey rode on and plowed into the caboose of the freight train. Had Casey jumped, he might have lived, but many others would have been killed. As it was, he sacrificed his life for those of his passengers and crew. The only casualty was Casey and the only injuries were a few bumps and bruises on those aboard his train. Legend has it that they found Casey's body with his hand still gripping the whistle cord.

OPPOSITE: If a train made an unscheduled stop, the crew had to protect the train from others following on the same track. To accomplish this, the conductor laid an explosive warning torpedo, as a brakeman ran back flagging a visual warning.

Casey Jones

Wallace Saunders's ballad of Casey Jones:

ABOVE: *Fast passenger trains required powerful locomotives. Casey Jones's new assignment brought with it a new engine with tall wheels that allowed for very high speeds. OPPOSITE: Long before he was immortalized for his heroic and tragic death, Casey Jones was a popular engineer among his fellow railroaders.*

Come all you rounders if you want to hear

The story told of a brave engineer;

Casey Jones was the rounder's name,

A high right-wheeler of mighty fame.

Caller called Casey about half-past four;

He kissed his wife at the station door,

Climbed into the cab with his orders in his hand,

Says, "This is my trip to the Holy Land."

Through South Memphis yards on the fly,

He heard the fireman say, "You got a white eye."

All the switchmen knew by the engine's moan

That the man at the throttle was Casey Jones.

It had been raining some five or six weeks;

The railroad tracks was like the bed of creek.

They rated him down to a thirty mile-gait—

Threw the southbound mail some eight hours late.

Fireman says, "Casey, you're running too fast.

You ran the block board the last station we passed."

Casey says, "Yes, I believe we'll make it through,

For she steams better than ever I knew."

Casey says, "Fireman, don't you fret.

Keep knocking at the fire door; don't give up yet.

I'm going to run her till she leaves the rail

Or make it on time with the southern mail."

Around the curve and down the dump,

Two locomotives were bound to bump.

Fireman hollered, "Casey, it's just ahead!

We might jump and make it, but we'll be dead!"

'Twas round this curve he spied a passenger train.

Rousing his engine, he caused the bell to ring.

Fireman jumped off, but Casey stayed on.

He's a good engineer, but he's dead and gone.

Poor Casey Jones was all right,

For he stuck to his duty both day and night.

They loved to hear the whistle and ring of No. 3

As he came into Memphis on the old I.C.

Headaches and heartaches and all kinds of pain

Are not apart from a railroad train.

Tales that are earnest, noble and grand

Belong to the life of a railroad man.

Kate Shelley—Saving the Midnight Express

One hot July evening in 1881, a great storm was brewing over central Iowa. Towering clouds swelled miles into the sky as the sun set, and distant thunder rolled, foreshadowing the storm to come. Farmers corralled their livestock and prepared for the rapidly approaching storm. Then in the evening, the wind picked up and rain fell in torrents. Lightning flashed across the sky and gale force winds howled across the landscape. The sky opened up and it poured and poured, drowning the land. Creeks swelled and rivers raged. The great power of rushing water knows no boundaries; trees were uprooted and small barns swept off their foundations to be carried downstream. As midnight approached, the storm abated and a calm began to set in.

Near the center of the storm area lay the Des Moines River Valley, a narrow but relatively deep swath in the otherwise rolling farmland. Near the town of Boone, the Chicago & North Western Railroad crossed the valley on its way west to the town of Council Bluffs, where it connected with the Union Pacific. With the completion of the transcontinental railroad to the Pacific in 1869, the C&NW line across Iowa had become a crucial thoroughfare for the movement of people and goods to the West.

On this terrible evening, C&NW's "Midnight Express"—its colloquial name—was making its way across Iowa, undeterred by the storm. The railroad runs in all weather, and while precautions are taken to avoid accidents, express trains are rarely laid up merely because of a fierce storm. The railroad crossed the Des Moines River on a long bridge and traveled over dozens of smaller streams by wooden trestles. As a precaution, during this storm, the railroad had dispatched a lone locomotive to inspect the track and check the condition of its bridges.

A few miles from Boone, on the west side of the Des Moines River Valley, some passengers waited out the storm at the Moingona depot. As midnight approached, the storm abated, the rain let

OPPOSITE: Rising above the predawn mists in the Des Moines River valley is Chicago & North Western's great steel high bridge named in honor of young Kate Shelley, who risked her life in a terrible storm to save a passenger train.

up, and the lightning, wind, and thunder rolled east. Relieved that the great storm had finally ended, they were anticipating the passage of the Midnight Express, which was overdue, probably delayed by the storm. Normally this express did not stop at lowly Moingona, but rolled right on through. Passengers at this station were served by less important local trains.

Suddenly an unexpected visitor appeared at the station: a frantic young woman with wild, wind-blown hair who was tattered and bruised and drenched to the skin. Gripping a smashed railway lantern she screamed to them, almost incoherently, "Stop the Express! Honey Creek Bridge is out!"

They did not know what to make of this strange apparition. Who was this crazy girl wandering around alone on such a stormy night? Was she mad? The station agent, hearing a commotion, came out to the platform; he immediately recognized the girl. She was young Kate Shelley, the eldest child of poor Michael Shelley, an Irishman who had worked as a railroad section hand, maintaining a section of the railroad with his crew, until he was tragically killed a few years earlier. Kate and her siblings lived with their mother near the tracks on the far side of the valley. She relayed her frantic message to the agent, and he immediately understood the gravity of the situation. Acting swiftly, he stopped the approaching express train at the station, preventing it from reaching the bridge. To a now awestruck audience, a weary Kate relayed her heroic story.

As the storm had raged outside, Kate and her mother had heard the lone engine, sent to look for damage, come down the valley and ease cautiously onto the Honey Creek bridge. Honey Creek, normally placid, had become a raging torrent; however, neither the Shelleys nor the train crew were aware that the creek had seriously undermined the railroad bridge.

Said Kate, "I heard the bell toll twice distinctly as [the engine] swayed on the uprooted bridge, and then came the horrible crash and the fierce hissing of steam as tender and engine went down in 25 feet (7.6m) of water." These horrible sounds had been followed by an eerie silence. Kate sprung into action. The Midnight Express was due soon, and if she did not warn someone, it too

would crash at Honey Creek and many people might be killed. She knew she must go to the depot, despite the peril, and stop the Express before it was too late. So she made her way out into the storm, lighting the way with her father's railroad lantern. She made her way to site of the crash and saw that at least two men had survived the wreck by clinging to trees. The bridge was impassable, forcing her to walk overland through the gloom to the Des Moines River Bridge, a considerable distance away.

Less hardy souls may have ended their journey right there on the flooded shore of the Des Moines. The railroad bridge's 500-foot (152.4m) span was her only means of traversing the river and attempting to cross it presented a threefold peril. There were no walkways on the bridge; it had be crossed by carefully balancing on the open tracks, which were wet and very slippery. If a train came while she was on the bridge there was no place to go but down. Furthermore, the river was a raging maelstrom of water and debris now almost level with the railhead. Despite the grave danger, Kate selflessly pressed on, crossing the bridge in the midst of the storm. At one point she slipped and fell, smashing the lantern and losing the only light she had. The bridge shuddered from the strain of the raging waters below. Knowing the Express might cross the span at any moment, she continued ahead, crawling on her hands and knees, tearing her clothing and bruising her skin.

Despite these formidable conditions, Kate made it across the river, and saved the Express and with it countless lives. A party was dispatched to rescue the hapless crew that had crashed through the Honey Creek Bridge. The two men Kate had seen after the crash were saved, but two others had been washed downstream and drowned.

ABOVE: A steam locomotive passes in the night.

In no time Kate Shelley became a national heroine. Every newspaper in the nation told her story. But following her adventure, Kate fell extremely ill and was confined to bed for three months. Later she was awarded a medal for her bravery, and the Chicago & North Western expressed its gratitude by giving her $500 (a considerable sum at a time when a dollar a day was considered a living wage) and a lifetime railroad pass. When she was older the railroad offered her employment at the Moingona Station. She accepted and became one of their few female agents. In 1900, the railroad bypassed its original crossing of the Des Moines Valley and built an enormous double-track steel trestle a half mile (.8km) long—the largest in the world at time of its completion. It was named the Kate Shelley High Bridge in her honor, and today if you visit Boone, road signs will direct you to this bridge.

ABOVE: A little girl looks on as a small steam locomotive pulls a passenger consist across a spindly trestle bridge, seemingly in defiance of gravity and perhaps even good sense.

A Picturesque Thousand Words

"*There were good talkers among the engineers of those days [1850s and 1860s], who were not afraid to express in language, often more expressive than polite, what they thought in favor of their own engines or in disparagement of others, and many a summer day was made warmer as a group of engineers on the shady side of the roundhouse whittled, bragged and bantered each other.*"

—Angus Sinclair, author of
Development of the Locomotive Engine

RIGHT: As an October morning dawns and the fog slowly lifts over Rockhill Furnace, Pennsylvania, East Broad Top's engine crew prepares their locomotive for another day of hard work.

The Pullman Porter

During the heyday of railroad travel in North America, most long-distance intercity passenger trains carried sleeping cars (specially equipped railroad cars with beds and other accommodations). While a few railroads maintained their own, most were kept up by companies that specialized in the construction and servicing of railroad sleepers. The largest, best-known, and longest-lasting of these firms was the Pullman Company. It was founded by George Pullman, a man whose name will be forever associated with the railroad sleeper and who treated his employees in a manner described alternately as feudalistic or paternalistic, depending on whose version of labor history you read.

Aboard sleeping cars, passengers were attended to by porters. The porter was stereotyped as a well-mannered, finely groomed black man. While porters generally took great pride in their profession, they were usually grossly underpaid for the important service they provided. Viewed through the more progressive lens of contemporary sociocultural mores, the image of the black porter seems racist and demeaning, but in the early twentieth century a job on the railroad was one of the few good employment opportunities available to African Americans.

ABOVE: The Pullman porter was a ubiquitous sight along platforms throughout the golden age of passenger trains. Although most porters were indeed black (because whites considered such work beneath them), railroad service was one of the few avenues to the middle class for African Americans at the time.

George

The first Pullman car was used by First Lady Mary Todd Lincoln, when she accompanied the slain President Lincoln back to Springfield, Illinois: the exposure secured the future of the Pullman Company. From 1875 to 1947, the Pullman Palace Car Co. made and equipped the majority of the sleeping cars used in the United States. The Pullman name came to symbolize sleeping-car service in North America to such an extent that it became customary for passengers to address all Pullman porters as "George."

RIGHT: A deluxe Pullman Palace car provided rail travelers with every conceivable amenity. Each car was decorated in the style of a Victorian parlor. Even first class on a 747 jet plane doesn't compare to this!

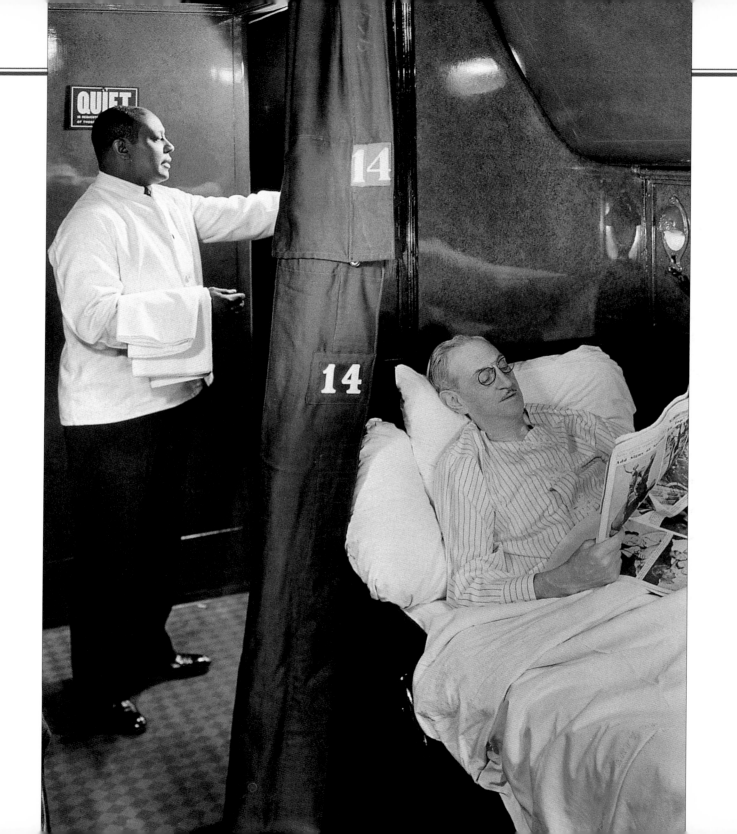

A Porter's Life

by W.C. Robinson, from *Folklore of Australian Railways*, by Patsy Adam Smith

Cleaning cars—polishing brass

Sweeping brakes and cleaning glass

Juggling samples—pushing brooms

Cleaning points and sweeping rooms

Chasing trucks around the yard

Waiting on a big fat guard

Nipping tickets—collecting freights

Shining scales and cleaning weights

Unloading trucks—folding sheets

Trimming lands and dusting seats

Climbing signals—trimming wicks

Using shovels, rakes and picks

Turning cheese knobs—shunting trains

Dodging showers when it rains

Pulling staffs—hurling hoops

Loading fowl and chicken coops

Loading wools and weighing trucks

Handling turkeys, geese and ducks

Dodging bosses—watching rails

Loading parcels, goods and mails

Selling tickets, weighing logs

Waybilling Prams, goats and dogs

Climbing ladders without fear

Filling tanks and loading beer

Pushing pens—answering phones

Filing numbers, labeling bones

Filling tenders up with water

Now who wouldn't be a Porter?

OPPOSITE: The Pullman porter played a vital role on U.S. passenger trains. He ensured that passengers were comfortable, turned down beds, woke people in time for their stations, and maintained a pleasant decorum.

Appearances

The following extracts are from the Wagner Palace Car Company staff manual of 1898:

Personal Appearance: Avoid putting hands in pockets in tails of uniform over-coats in cold weather, giving employee a rather loafering appearance, as well as spreading the tail of the coats and getting them out of shape.

Collars and cuffs: White linen only—celluloid are prohibited.

Maids: Will wear the prescribed uniform while on duty, and must at all times carry sufficient linen for the round trip. They must also have the following equipment: Book of Rules, set of keys, bottle of smelling salts, liquid camphor, black and white thread, package of needles, and box of assorted pins for ladies' use. Maids must be extremely careful to maintain a proper deportment while on duty. Under no circumstances will they allow any familiarity on the part of the crew or passengers, and they should at all times avoid even the appearance of it. No excuse will be accepted for any violation of this rule.

OPPOSITE: Many railroads prided themselves on their cuisine, and the quality of food in the diner was often a defining element of service aboard a luxury passenger train. Passengers might select one line over another just because of the diner menu.

The Conductor

While the locomotive engineer controlled the engine, the conductor was in charge of the train. On passenger trains he was responsible not only for collecting tickets but also for finding fare evaders and stowaways. Those caught riding without a ticket were at his mercy. Robert Louis Stevenson, the Scottish author, who in 1879 rode across the United States by train, wrote of an incident on board a train he was riding through the Midwest on his way to California:

At a place called Creston, a drunken man got [on board]. He was aggressively friendly, but, according to English notions, not at all unpresentable upon a train. For one stage he eluded the notice of officials; but just as we were beginning to move out of the next station, Cromwell by name, by came the conductor. There was a word or two of talk; and then the official had the man by the shoulders, twitched him from his seat, marched him through the car, and sent him flying on to the track. It was done in three motions, as exact as a piece of drill. The train was still moving slowly, although beginning to mend her pace, and the drunkard got to his feet without a fall. . . . The conductor stood on the steps with one hand on his hip, looking back at him; and perhaps this attitude imposed upon the creature, for he turned without further ado, and went staggering along the tracks toward Cromwell.

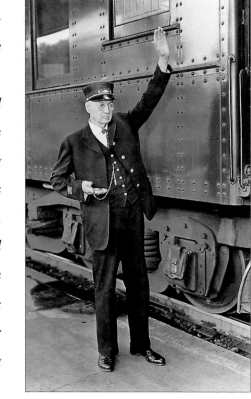

OPPOSITE: In the early twentieth century many long-distance passenger trains began carrying open-observation lounge cars, where passengers could relax and watch the miles roll by. RIGHT: The locomotive engineer often caught the imagination of young boys and songwriters, but the conductor actually called the shots: he was the one in charge of the train.

I've Been Working on the Railroad

I've been working on the railroad
All the livelong day,
I've been working on the railroad
To pass the time away.
Don't you hear the whistle blowing?
Rise up so early in the morn.
Don't you hear the captain shouting,
"Dinah blow your horn."

RIGHT: It took a lot of people doing many jobs to make a railroad run smoothly. Here, a man in the control booth keeps his eye on the rails for incoming trains. The enormous levers in front of him probably controlled the track switches. OPPOSITE: Maintaining accurate time could mean the difference between life and death. Railroaders synchronized their pocket watches with company clocks daily to insure consistent time across the railroad.

Chapter Five

WRONG TURNS

INCIDENTS AND ACCIDENTS

Sadly, unusual, unfortunate, and tragic events tend to make the most interesting tales. Train stories are no exception. While railway employees, management, and passengers prefer that trains arrive at their destinations on time and without incident, storytellers thrive on the drama of trains involved in much less routine activity. How dull it would be if this book were filled with happy accounts of trains leaving their terminals, stopping routinely to pick up passengers, and arriving safely, without trauma or tragedy! Spectacular crashes, wild runaways, and malicious train robberies are the highlights of railroad lore.

PAGE 105: Railway men risked their lives every day. This Pennsy derailment in Chicago on September 17, 1941, cost the life of the locomotive engineer and seriously injured the fireman.
OPPOSITE: Clearing mountain rails of snow was a routine but dangerous business. A Canadian Pacific crew poses with their plow among enormous drifts in the Selkirk Range. RIGHT: A typical grade crossing—this one along the Union Pacific at Modena, Utah—alerts motorists that extreme care should be taken when crossing the tracks. Hundreds die every year in railway grade crossing accidents, most caused by inattentive drivers.

Avalanche!

Canadian Pacific's transcontinental mainline traverses the Selkirk Mountains in British Columbia by way of a treacherous crossing at Rogers Pass. There are numerous tragic tales about the building and operation of the railways through this snowy crevice. The line was completed in the 1880s and was still a dangerous run more than twenty years later. One of the worst stories still inspires fear in the hearts of even the most hardened winter railroaders.

On the evening of March 5, 1910, a Canadian Pacific plow crew was attempting to clear a snow slide that had blocked the tracks in front of a westbound passenger train when a tremendous avalanche roared down the mountain. An incredible roar and a fierce blast of icy wind preceded thousands of tons of snow tumbling down the mountainside. Men and equipment, including a 100-ton (110t) rotary snowplow, were swept away by the torrent of snow. Bodies and machines were carried for hundreds of feet as the snow cascaded some 1,500 feet (457.2m) below rail level, into Bear Creek. The locomotive assigned to push the plow was demolished. However, not everything went down; in the churning tumult of the avalanche, the plow was actually carried up, and it landed on the roof of a showshed designed to protect the tracks. Of the sixty-three men at the scene all but one perished, most suffocating to death under tons of snow. Although the railroad dispatched hundreds of men to search for victims, many bodies were never recovered. The one survivor is said to have quit the railroad upon his recovery. It was among the worst tragedies in Canadian railroad history.

OPPOSITE: Snow is a formidable obstacle, and a train bogged down in deep snow can be stuck for days. Even in modern times there are harrowing tales of trains caught in mountain storms.

Wreck of the Old 97

The original song was by either Charles Noell or Henry Clay Work; it is unclear which of these men actually wrote it.

Well, they gave him his orders at Monroe, Virginia,

Saying, "Steve you are way behind time.

This is not thirty-eight, it's old ninety-seven.

You must put her into Spencer on time."

He turned and said to this black greasy fireman,

"Just shovel on a little more coal,

and when we cross the White Oak Mountain

you can watch old ninety-seven roll."

It's a mighty rough road from Lynchburg to Danville

On the line there's a three-mile grade,

It was on this grade that he lost his airbrake,

You can see what a jump he made.

He was going down the grade making ninety miles an hour,

when his whistle broke into a scream.

They found him in the wreckage, his hand on the throttle,

he was scalded to death by the steam.

Now, ladies take warning,

from this time now on learn,

never speak harsh words to your true loving husband,

he may leave you and never return.

OPPOSITE: Flash floods can mean disaster for a railroad: tracks can be undermined by the rivers running alongside, and may even be swept away entirely.

Federal Runaway

On January 15, 1953, Pennsylvania Railroad streamlined electric locomotive GG1 No. 4876 was leading the *Federal* to Washington, D.C., from Boston. The *Federal* was an express that left Boston in the evening and arrived in Washington in the early morning. On this particular trip, the train had been delayed several times because of difficulties with its air brakes. But the problems apparently had all been solved and the train was making good time over Pennsylvania's high-speed mainline with a full load of passengers, many of whom were planning to attend President-elect Dwight Eisenhower's inauguration.

Nearing the destination, Washington's Union Station, a terminal with mostly stubend tracks (those that end at the station), locomotive engineer Harry Brower routinely applied the train brakes. To his horror, they failed and would not slow his speeding train. He made a desperate effort to stop the train by dumping the air—an emergency brake application—but to no avail. The engine brake was virtually useless with a heavy passenger train rolling along behind, and, making matters worse, the tracks go down a short grade just before the terminal. The *Federal* was a runaway and there was no stopping it!

As the train raced toward destiny, Brower blasted a harrowing warning on the locomotive's horn—a loud, low, grating sound, distinct to the GG1 electrics. Towermen who controlled the switches that routed trains into the terminal were alerted by the signal. They had only seconds to act, and there was little they could do. The *Federal* was headed right toward the station! One smart towerman called the station agent, whose office lay directly in the path of the racing train, yelling, "We have a runaway!" The agent wasted no time and ran from his office just as the locomotive crashed through the bumper at the end of the track, flew into the station, and demolished the office and a newsstand. For a moment the train came to rest in the main concourse, then, under the great

OPPOSITE:On the morning of January 15, 1953, the Federal *lost its brakes and came crashing into Washington's Union Station. The mighty Pennsylvania Railroad GG1 electric 4876 leans into the basement after the notorious crash.*

ABOVE: One of the most famous disasters in North American railroad history did not result in any fatalities. Fortunately, the station was nearly empty at the time of the terrible Federal wreck.

strain of the 460,000-pound (208, 840 kg) locomotive, the floor collapsed, and the huge streamliner sank into the basement of the station. Miraculously, no one was killed in the tremendous crash, although there were some minor injuries.

The next day all the papers carried photographs of Pennsylvania 4876 slanted at a sharp angle, one end deep into the basement of the station. It was truly an amazing crash. It was also a testiment to the rugged design of the GG1 electric locomotive, which had been built with crew safety in mind. Number 4876 was removed from the basement in pieces, brought back to the railroad's shops, reassembled, and repainted. It served the railroad and its successors for another thirty years before being retired in 1983. Today the locomotive is preserved in Baltimore and someday may be restored for public display.

Appeasing the Spirits

Kenya Railways requires that all trains stop for several minutes before crossing a dam in the southern part of this African country. The practice was adopted on the advice of local residents after several mysterious derailments on the Mwatate Dam were blamed on evil spirits that are said to inhabit the resevoir. Townsfolk claimed that the spirits were angered when the trains moved across the dam without first appeasing them by stopping in tribute.

RIGHT: As automobiles and highway travel became the predominant form of transportation in North America, many railways were closed and abandoned. Often the tracks were slowely reclaimed by nature.

Five Miles for a Hat

The Algoma Central is a line in western Ontario that runs north from Sault Saint Marie, on the straits between Lakes Superior and Michigan, deep into the Canadian wilderness. In his book *Algoma Central Railway,* O.S. Nock, who has written numerous books about railroading around the world, relates a humorous tale that occurred in the early days of this remote line railway, sometime shortly after the turn of the century.

One day, the journey of a southbound passenger train was stopped abruptly, and the train began backing up—an unorthodox maneuver that was not in accordance with the train schedule. Apparently a passenger had stuck her head out a window and lost her prized hat when it blew off her head. In most circumstances the hat would have remained lost, but an exception was made in this particular case. The woman was the conductor's girlfriend, and he used his authority to insist that the train reverse and the hat be retrieved. His lady would not be without her hat if he had a say in the matter, and he did! After some five miles (8km) in reverse, the hat was indeed discovered—although a large stuffed bird that had been mounted on it was nowhere to be found—and the journey resumed.

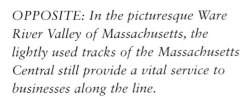

OPPOSITE: *In the picturesque Ware River Valley of Massachusetts, the lightly used tracks of the Massachusetts Central still provide a vital service to businesses along the line.*

"Lost at Gloucester"

The distance between the inside faces of the rails is called the "gauge," and agreement on this size of distance has been critical to the development of railroads throughout the world. When each railway was built privately, builders used whatever gauge was most convenient to them, and it was necessary to change cars at places on the rails where the gauge changed. The problems associated with the transfer of goods at the points of "break of gauge" were quite severe almost from the beginning. In England, a differential between broad and standard gauge at Gloucester necessitated a complete train change, with passengers, crew, and baggage all changing cars. Much was lost in the resultant confusion, and these mishaps inspired a popular expression: "Lost at Gloucester," which became the universal explanation for anything mislaid on the British rail system.

OPPOSITE: The excitement of boarding a passenger train is a timeless thrill offering the possibility of endless adventure. At one time trains went nearly everywhere.

The Great Train Chase

During times of war, railroads assumed a crucial strategic role transporting troops, equipment, and munitions, as well as war prisoners and civilians. Railroads changed the very way wars were waged. With trains, troops could be deployed and moved faster and in greater numbers than ever before. An overland march that may have taken days prior to the advent of the railroad might require only a couple of hours on a train. A nation with a strong railroad network had a distinct advantage over an adversary with a weak network. Countries that failed to adopt a single standard gauge would find the resulting inflexibility crippling. The inability to transfer supplies and people quickly from one place to another could easily make the difference between winning and losing a battle. Naturally, the strategic importance of railroads also meant they were prime military targets.

One of the most famous railroad events of all time is a story of attempted wartime sabotage, an event now known universally as the Great Train Chase. In April 1862, during the American Civil War—among the first major conflicts in which railroads held a decisive role—a band of Union agents under the leadership of one James J. Andrews seized Western & Atlantic's *General* at Big Shanty, Georgia, and raced northward through Confederate territory. Their mission was twofold: to steal a valuable wartime machine—a steam locomotive—and to wreak havoc on the Western & Atlantic by destroying tracks, severing telegraph lines, and burning bridges. The mission did not go well for the Union invaders. Their party was hotly pursued by Confederate forces and ultimately subdued before they could do substantive damage to the railroad or escape to Union territory. Andrews and several of his followers were caught and hung. Yet the intent of their mission reveals the crucial nature of the railroad in the bloody Civil War.

OPPOSITE: In April 1862, Union raiders seized Western & Atlantic's General, *a handsome and powerful American-type locomotive. Their mission was foiled: the locomotive was hotly pursued, the* General *was recovered, and the raiders were captured.*

Tay Bridge Disaster

As the growing rail system stretched north into Scotland, two great barriers, the wide estuaries of the Firth of Forth and the Firth of Tay, 40 miles (64km) apart, blocked the direct route from Edinburgh to Dundee and Aberdeen. The Forth was first bridged at Stirling, where it narrowed to a river, but a long detour west was required before the Tay could be crossed.

A great competition was brewing between the east and west coast routes to the popular vacation destinations of the Scottish Highlands, and the Tay detour via Perth was causing enough delay to negate the advantage of the eastern line. In the growing competition for holiday traffic, speed was everything. Ferries transferred passengers across the firths for a time, but to the North British Railway, it was obvious that the Tay would have to be bridged.

Engineer Thomas Bouch produced a design for a tall, slender cast- and wrought-iron viaduct that would carry the North British Line directly into Dundee. The 2-mile (3.2km) bridge, among the longest railway bridges in the world, was opened for passenger traffic on June 1, 1878. Unfortunately, the design was not particularly skillful—in fact, Bouch calculated the lateral wind loading at just 10 pounds per square foot (50kg per square meter), which was hopelessly inadequate. To compound matters, the workmanship was poor, and the quality of the cast-iron columns supporting the bridge was deplorable.

On the night of December 28, 1879, during a fierce gale, the North British Railway *Edinburgh Mail* crept slowly across the bridge. The high girders forming the center of the bridge swayed and then began to tear apart. The entire train, carrying seventy-five passengers, plunged into the stormy water. There were no survivors. Many victims' bodies were never recovered.

OPPOSITE: In an especially harrowing disaster, an entire train was swept off the Tay Bridge and into the water.

Patrick Matthew, a contemporary who is now known as the seer of Gourdie, is credited with having predicted the Tay Bridge disaster when he said: "In the case of accident with a heavy train on the bridge, the whole of the passengers will be killed. The eels will come out to gloat in delight over the horrible wreck and banquet."

A second Tay Bridge—built far more sturdily than the first—was completed in June 1887.

ABOVE: The wrecked remains of the locomotive that hauled the ill-fated train over the Tay were later pulled from the watery depths.

Two Blocked Trains

(sung to the music of "Three Blind Mice")

from *Folklore of Australian Railways*, by Patsy Adam Smith

Two blocked trains,

Two blocked trains,

    See where they stand,

    See where they stand,

They both are waiting to be let through,

Some passengers swear till they're black & blue,

And others drink whiskey, or bill and coo!!

    On the two blocked trains.

RIGHT: A train of the Denver & Rio Grande rolls along the Arkansas River through the confines of the Royal Gorge, west of Cañon City, Colorado.

Index

Photo Credits

Bibliography

Adams, Ramon F. *The Language of the Railroader.* Norman, Oklahoma: University of Oklahoma Press, 1977.

Alvarez, Eugene. *Travel on Southern Antebellum Railroads, 1828–1860.* University, Alabama: University of Alabama Press, 1974.

Anderson, Frank W. *Frontier Guide to the Incredible Rogers Pass.* Canada: Frontier Books, 1968.

Beebe, Lucius. *20th Century.* Berkeley, California: Howell-North, 1962.

Berton, Pierre. *The Last Spike: The Great Railway 1881–1885.* Toronto: McClelland and Stewart Limited, 1971.

Black, Robert C. III. *The Railroads of the Confederacy.* Chapel Hill, North Carolina: University of North Carolina Press, 1952.

Carlson, Robert E. *The Liverpool & Manchester Railway Project 1821–1831.* New York: Augustus M. Kelley Publishers, 1969.

Casey, Robert J., and W.A.S. Douglas. *The Lackawanna Story.* New York: McGraw-Hill, 1951.

Dale, Rodney. *Early Railways.* New York: Oxford University Press, 1994.

Douglas, George H. *All Aboard! The Railroad in American Life.* New York: Paragon House, 1992.

Erbseon, Wayne. *Singing Rails: Railroadin' Songs, Jokes & Stories.* Asheville, North Carolina: Native Ground Music, 1997.

Faith, Nicholas. *Locomotion; the Railway Revolution.* London: BBC Books, 1993.

Holbrook, Stewart H. *The Story of American Railroads.* New York: Crown Publishers, 1947.

———. *James J. Hill.* New York: Alfred A. Knopf, 1955.

Hoyt, Edwin P. *The Vanderbilts and their Fortunes.* New York: Doubleday & Company, 1962.

Hubbard, Freeman. *Great Trains of All Time.* New York: Grosset & Dunlap, 1962.

———. *Railroad Avenue.* New York: McGraw-Hill, 1946.

Husband, J. *The Story of the Pullman Car.* Chicago: A.C. McClurg, 1917.

Jensen, Oliver. *The American Heritage History of Railroads in America.* New York: American Heritage Publishing, 1975.

Kirby, Maurice W. *The Origins of Railway Enterprise.* Cambridge: Cambridge University Press, 1993.

Malone, Michael P. *James J. Hill: Empire Builder of the Northwest.* Norman, Oklahoma: University of Oklahoma Press, 1996.

Marshall, John. *The Guinness Railway Book.* Enfield, Middlesex, England: Guinness Books, 1989.

Nock, O.S. *Algoma Central Railway.* London: Adam & Charles Black, 1975

Riley, C.J. *The Encyclopedia of Trains & Locomotives.* New York: Michael Friedman Publishing Group, 1994.

Sinclair, Angus. *Development of the Locomotive Engine.* New York: 1907.

Skeat, W.O. *George Stephenson; The Engineer and His Letters.* London: The Institution of Mechanical Engineers, 1973.

Stevenson, Robert Louis. *Across the Plains.* New York: Charles Scribner's Sons, 1897.

Tupper, Harmon. *To the Great Ocean: Siberia and the Trans-Siberian Railway.* Boston: Little, Brown & Company, 1965.

Vauclain, Samuel M., and Earl Chapin May. *Steaming Up!* New York: Brewer & Warren, 1930.

Ziel, Ron. *Steel Rails to Victory.* New York: Hawthorn Books, 1970.

Zimmermann, Karl R. *The Remarkable GG1.* New York: Quadrant Press, 1977.